Into
the *Matrix*
of *Insights*

Into
the *Matrix*
of *Insights*

Beyond a Dream-Borne Jet Lag

By

SHUKLA BHATTACHARYA

RESOURCE *Publications* · Eugene, Oregon

Resource Publications
An Imprint of Wipf and Stock Publishers
199 W. 8th Ave., Suite 3
Eugene, OR 97401

www.wipfandstock.com

PAPERBACK ISBN: 978-1-6667-6412-3
HARDCOVER ISBN: 978-1-6667-6413-0
EBOOK ISBN: 978-1-6667-6414-7

VERSION NUMBER 021523

To those sublime minds that have discovered their soul's calling—have nerved themselves to spreading the bliss of endearment and altruistic benevolence. To Poetic geniuses— the paragons of abstract reasoning, psychic attunement. To the good-humored and the tolerant, the pure-hearted and the principled, the brainiac and the maniac, besides all those striving for self transformation in prisons and correctional homes … irrespective of their vocation.

How can you prove whether at this moment we are sleeping, and all our thoughts are a dream; or whether we are awake, and talking to one another in the waking state?

—PLATO

I want to know all Gods thoughts; all the rest are just details.

—ALBERT EINSTEIN

If you believe that your thoughts originate inside your brain, do you also believe that television shows are made inside your television set?

—WARREN ELLIS

Contents

Preface

My experience of soaking up the expression *Poetic genius* is beyond any theoretical understanding of the term, and I have ever been enthralled by the realm of this eternal enigma. No wonder thus, during every single saga of life, it's the poet's pen that stole the space of my consciousness and thought, consistently captivated both my reasoning potential and power of imagination, emerging with the possibilities of a panacea, a tell-tale embodying ecstasy.

Acknowledgements

No matter what I say, I would hardly ever be able to express an iota of my veneration for the Mystical One Above. Hence, I choose not to make any attempt to dilute my depth of Gratitude to the Supreme Being.

I am, indeed, beyond delighted to extend my Countless Thanks to Matt Wimer- the distinctly well-disposed, gracious Managing Editor, George Callihan—one of the most obliging, remarkably supportive Editorial Administrators, and every single diligent member of the Publishing Team at Wipf and Stock- USA.

My unfeigned, unshakeable Thanks go to Dr. Alan Corkish, Editor; Erbacce Press- UK, my exemplary parents; God sent hubby; angelic mother-in-law who's no more; noble, versatile only brother… among a myriad of kind souls- who so tenderly thought, I *am* their *Voice*.

Introduction

If I speak straight from the shoulder, I am rather bemused as to how I should write an Introduction for this book. Far as I can recall, it has been written by virtue of the unique coalescing of a still small voice, a sense of conscious reasoning, a resolute celestial segment of solitude, an attachment with detachment inclination, an inadvertent embodying of Spinozistic cognition- especially his *scientia intuitiva* or knowledge of the *third kind*, and my idiosyncratic imbibing of the theories of love … that involve substantial evolving over the last three decades.

I would like to humbly suggest, please do not flip through the pages of this book if you're not rich enough to embrace the glory of thy penury … despite living precariously for ages. Please do not flip through the pages of this book if you're not rich enough to forgo the dreams of thy deep pockets … despite rolling in money ever since you were born.

In a robotically advancing post pandemic period of breathing space crisis like the present, I would go further and say that understanding the reason why I wrote what I wrote in the paragraph above, is rendered all the more urgent because today we realize that we are, indeed, standing in the midst of a blind alley- almost a dead end- created by greed, cut-throat aggression, war, despotism, egotism, isolation, angst, and an abiding sense of loss- seeking salvation in a futile pursuit of happiness.

I do not expect accolades in the sense that a majority of the readers will be moved … but I do hope that there at least will be some instances of perceptive minds that might be intrigued to a certain level, inspired to think.

It may be just a Hut

It may be just a Hut
By the countryside
But …
Well-equipped
With accessories
Mandatory for modern homes.

Here,
Interior decoration involves
Influx of Oxygen,
Wooden floors winking at Woodpeckers,
Doozle little doors
Swinging with the Skies.

A mini Pond at the backyard-
Flaunting Lotuses and Lilies,
The latest Natural Spa
That's not really silly!

Trees surround tall
To tame the heat,
With its Green Grass Lawn
Pulling People from the streets!

While strolling along the lawn
Their Depression Heals,
While a huge Laughter Club
The silence steals!

A look at the hut
Brings back the Bards,
Of Smiles sending signals
To those drifted apart!

Where crazy curtains creek
By scrolling flakes of bamboo,
With every single flake
Sharing stories of déjà vu!

Loyalty

There's a crisis of trust
These days-
Suspicion overrules.

This in turn
Imprisons the innocent
Locks up love life
Burns bridges
Sells self worth
Coins questions-
On: Dependability.

A vigilant street dog
Running on a rainy night
Reminds of
Lessons learnt
On Loyalty
Long long back.

Space

Even the Space
Might not be enough
For monsters
To feast on
The eternal scope
Of space: in human souls.

Scot Kelly, help!
Catch the beasts
In thy camera- Catch!
Let's make space
For the space in our souls,
Once again.

Connectivity

Infinite Numeric
With Alluring Letters,
Towering Technology
With the brain that matters,
Combine to choreograph-

A cutting edge of connectivity;
Recreating a replica
Of recreational repertoire-
Revolving around:
The basic instinct to belong.

Past Un-passed

The intoxicating fragrance of yester years
Sealed inside
The soul-stirring fun of innocence
Kisses goodbye
To the infuriating fumes of existing maladies.

You and I nowhere now-
Floating aside are the scintillating reflections of
A foolishly simple and maddening lost world …
Where …
Involuntary cardiac muscles
And
Metamorphosed tear glands
Constantly ground the framework for
An excruciatingly Painful … Rhythmic Nostalgia.

Love Withdrawn

Those kind eyes
Once sketched my Skies
Of sacred sex
And silver nights,
Of mirrors that promised
To be all lights,
Of drizzling days
Yet sun so bright,
Of dreams and dance
That spoke of smiles …

Those kind eyes
Where art thou
Closed and charmed
By Austere vow …
Medicines- you said
Caused it all
The reason why
Euphoria stood tall.
Love at last, is now withdrawn-
My lifeline lost, my all is gone.

Would You still come?

Long after when you are gone
And I have slept for years,
One dark dawn
If you still come
To see me and my fears …
Then plant a kiss
On my forehead
Proud of this virgin …
Can she scent your
Thirst again
And haste to pull you back
For more?
Or will she choose to
Be a chaste
For thy next touch
To leave her and go?

Unsocial

When one of my
Once best friend
Called up from overseas …
To listen to my voice,
To tell about her nostalgia
For me- the friend long lost,
I said I believe in
Not being so social, you see …

Ignorantly unaware of
An upcoming insanity
That was planning to
Punish me,
I was so sure of myself …
Happily unapologetic.

Today my once best friend
Paid a Visit to me
Crossing all the miles.
Here I was,
Sitting secluded at an asylum
Eating my dirty nails,
That grew stale over the years.

She came to me
And wiped her tears.
Who said you're unsocial,

Look how you've pulled me here, she said.
That is because
You are social
Stupid- I said.

At sunset
It was time to leave
Like a sad mom
She said-
Sleep for now
O my dear
I will come again.

I saw the skies
Then held her tight
And hid her shoes
Out of my fright
Then locked the door
For that night
While crying like the rains.

Breaking News

White Lies
Have a first cousin:
White Norms.

Unlike other Norms,
White Norms
When broken-
Never bring Breaking News!

How do you break
The Broken- after all?
Non- whites seldom wonder.

Pleasure

Remembering
A sense of devotion
Mingled with faith
In words unspoken
Search eyes closed
Breaking barriers
And tears untold-
Just for a glance.

With that glance
All the turmoil
Would turn to an ocean
Of Oxygen-laden peace
And a tranquil smile
Promising Paradise.

Eyes in dreams
Still drink the opium
Of Pleasure.

Effervescence

Some people are made that way
They can't help it either.
Blame their education?
Blame their genes?
Blame their puerile impulse?
Or blame the boundaries
Baked in their brains
By the Master-Planner …

Some people are not really looking-
There must be a reason.
They laugh with Hyenas
Cry with crocodiles
But do not dance with Daffodils.
They can't help it either.

The Charm of Pain

You learn to laugh loud,
You tend to try more.
You learn to let go,
You gain a high score.
You learn to hide,
You latch a closed door.
You learn to feel lost,
You bang the hard floor.
Yet- you are loyal to the charm-
The charm in turn- Does no harm.

Minor Burns

Even if
Your entire community
Joins hands
To bring back the fire
That brought thee
O Wretched blisters-
It would not be enough to
Set my crematory-
My corpse has been
Lying there since ages.
Not a speck of ash
Could be squeezed …
All the smoke you see
Whistles out of my celebration:
The bubbling bonfire!
Get lost- You fools!

Vacuum

Barren seeds conceived by Eliot's Waste Land-
Buildings boast.
Beneath the basement
Cannibals have eaten up all-
Ruling over the curse
Of a Fatal appetite.

Above stands tall the left-over:
Ignorant- bold- dictating skyscrapers.
Or
Is it self-imposed rat-racing
Of cognition, meritorious insight, filtered compassion..?

A Sequel to Terrorism

The throttled victim
Advocates his innocence no more.
Moving by degrees little by little,
Re-conceptualizes.

Metaphysical verity unravels
With resonant reassurance:
The gruesome advent of Apathy.

Self reproach indoctrinates and
Nurtures the phoenix;
Intimidated by the latest prognosis.

Guilt pangs

Trauma over transgression
Soaked in the sponge of sweat and semen
Secretly segregates synapse and serotonin.

Sinner-syndrome
Subjugates the semantics of soul.
Sanity sunk.

Love life

Love lives-
Drinking Depression,
Seeking sacred shelter
In
A scrupulously silenced,
Secret, Sublime!

Know thyself

While it rains,
A desert desperately cries
To save its crooked cactus.
While it doesn't,
She drinks in the depths of despair
Of bearing barren blood.

Love-making

My sweetheart is, sleeping now-
Do you know, he looks like how?
An angel with closed lotus eyes,
Innocent face, divine 'n' wise!

My sweetheart is, just awake-
Where's his cup- of coffee 'n' cake?
While I hurry up- to serve it myself,
He sweetly seeks some other help!

You may've guessed it right-
What his wish could be,
Now in his arms,
Let me be me!

Different Worlds

When I open my eyes-
To see you,

           Flowers bloom
          -And beat my gloom
           Birds fly high
          -To see me in the sky!
           Butterflies dance
          -For just a glance!
           Rivers glow
          -While I flow!
           Dewdrops shine
          -And say they're mine!
           The sun is bright
          -Beheading my fright!
           The moon comes soon
          -As a big boon!
           Stars not far
          -With all-smiles bar!
           The sky bold blue
          -Trickling love true!

When I open my eyes-
To see you not,

           Those flowers dry
          -And see me cry;
           Birds don't hum
          -Seeing me mum;

Butterflies buzz
-And think that was;
Rivers stand still
-With sorrows filled;
Dews don't drop
-On land or crop;
The Sun silent
-And seems secretive;
The Moon morose
-As if I don't live;
Stars far away
-For a glance I fight;
Sky pale white
-And a cloudy night.

In Your Eyes

In your eyes
I have seen-
The ethereal promise
Of peeling the pivot of my pain;
And planting lush green leaves on my land.

In your eyes
I have seen-
The miracle manna
Purely meant for: My powerful moves
And deadly defense of dreams.

Shame

Why wasn't I beheaded with your's?
Perhaps I had no head at all-
And they could see
My headlessness
Tumbling down through ages.

What did they do to your head?
Crowned with a cruel jewel?
Or frowned at my fright
While proud of their might
Fanned their foul fuel?

My headless shame
Shrieks no more,
Laying Dead-sunk in
The stinking sick sea of
Severed souls.

What if

What if the henpecked
Hires a Hedgehog?
What if the docile
Becomes a Bull-dog?

What if one's fiancé
Equals a bad luck?
What if the beloved
Befriends a duck?

What, if a mother
Flirts with another?
What, if the father
Doesn't care to bother?

What, if- a merry-go-round
Goes gaga over google
Or feels homebound?
What if on earth- I shockingly find
I've finally lost-
All my mind?

As all that glitters is not gold,
And golden words are seldom told,
Explore thy soul

To see the manifold-
Before my friend,
You've grown too old.

Mother disclaimer

Distorted chirps
And chills of a child
Erupts into fury
Through the chimney of despair:
Mourning for the mother.

A Mad, Morose mother lays Clueless-
Moaning: in the midst of monstrous mountains.
Mammary glands manipulated
By the mesmerizing moves
Of smoking Marijuana.

Conscience

When I play with my ball
And hear Mamma call,
I try to fly-
But just then fall!

When I don't study,
Dad's no buddy.
I try to cry-
But that seems a lie!

When I'm dishonest,
My sister doesn't talk.
Away I walk-
But oh a stumbling block!

When I'm not humble,
My little brothers grumble.
I try to ignore-
But that's No Score!

What is this Conscience?
From where does she come?
When all else is burning-
She's glued to me like gum!

The Cursed Compromise

Whimpering words withering;
Faded fluctuations in fool's paradise
Slowly strengthened.

Subconscious substantiates:
Compromise cool, complacent.
Self seeking shoulder screams

Under the utopia
Of
Novel Narcissism.

Of No-Man's Land

Retrospection revitalizes the revolutionary.
Else, *might-have-been*-s might well migrate.
Amassing abstract ambivalence,
Alzheimer's mends a menacing- no man's land.

Beloved

No reason why
I should cry
Yet I do
With all pain true.

Is it all clear?
Or is it the fear?
Of losing you
In my dreams- new?

O! dear pain!
Just in vain
I said 'go'
Don't you know?

Take me there
Where all is fair
And you were born.
I won't see you- in pieces torn.

For now I know
I can Not let u go.
When u are not around
I have lost my ground.

O pain!
Not in vain
You live for me- I pray for thee,
If this is a lie- won't I die?

Poverty-stricken Passion

Mishandled Midas touch
From poverty-stricken passion
Waters the wealth of
Amazing altruism!
Ambience: anxiously ambiguous.

Aches

The convocation of Communalism.
Homicidal hoopla.
Heaps of hurt. Hysterics.

A mocking morale mops away
Multi-ethnic motivations.

Morbid mordant merry-making
Makes for a modest milch-cow.

Proudly Possessive

A polite possessor's personal premises plundered.
Poison prevails over the pensive.
Post-mortem postulates
Painstaking paintings of Phantom pride.

The Dictum of a Dilapidated Distance

Musing; Moaning;
Muzzy; Myopic.
Musty; Mundane
Murky-murmur.
Mayhem; Maverick mismatched
Mystique mother: misty-eyed.

Polluting Pebbles

Pieces of pissing around
Pin-prick and provoke pique;
Perturbed perverts perspire.
Pitying perseverance, placid.

Insatiable

Soaked seeds of sultry stations
Sing the sweetest songs of starvation.
Hunger heals in haste,
Bingeing on bereavement:
Bearing the banner of Beatitude.

Fun Crown

Starting with the junior most,
For ma'am Shagufta, we were host-
Chicken roast or *biryani gosht*,
Best of all is '*Baaji* ' toast!

Sweet Farzana and Nawreen,
Brilliant birds, with observations keen!
Three together, happy we had seen,
Cute Fatema, in the nest has been!

Chums Nadira, Shazia and Rubina,
Fruit 'n' flowers of music mania!
Sentimental, chirpy and caring for all,
Watch your words! Or tender tears fall!

Soft-spoken, rosy, dear Ambreen,
Not just Honey's, our queen you've been.
With patience and passion, busy as a bee,
Strong at will, how mild is she!

Beauty butterflies called Asma 'n' Mona,
Once thither, thence hither, '*duuur- nehi- hona!*'
Ask anyone 'n' you will be told,
With a few exceptions, 'old is gold'!

Naheed ma'am, Turjaboo 'n' *Aapaa* Hameeda ,
Welcomed us there at *koolia* Sabya-
Tea with snacks 'n' *Arbi* quite a while,
A worthy Dr. Naheed, lent a hand with smile!

Dear Dr. Rabeya, our jewel in the crown,
With you around, who could ever frown?
Wisdom you hide, wit by your side,
A high sense of humour, you fill us with pride!

Time for good-bye, says ma'am Shukla now,
Salaam, Ustad Ahlam! Forget u? How?
The holy chimes … of Saudi Arabia,
In silence sings … tunes that are dear.
O! Cheer-up all! While down memory lane,
The spring of pain flows time 'n' again.

On Misinterpretations

 I say I love
You say I don't
 I say I will
You say I won't.

I say 'See-
It's easy to cheat!'
You say 'That's-
No mean feat!'

I call it quits-
'With you won't dine.'
You never resign,
Look divine,
With calm and care,
Say 'You're mine!'

I say 'You bore!
Talk no more.'
You shut the door,
Sing Celtic lore,
Then shower your love
With a smiling roar.

How could I live
Ever without you?
How not love
Misinterpretations- a few?

Bastard Bastion

At your courtyard,
You take the freedom to choose:
Often, the alien.
Confessions of a Xenofile, says Amitabh Ghosh.

Far far away,
And even miles further,
I lie the alien, not the chosen one though.
Fabricated, framed, a flipping foe.

Soul mate

A celestial journey of twenty-one years
Delicately dissolved those fears,
Of self-sacrifice and remorse.

Now, to thee I bow with all head bent.
A regular rhythm of breathlessness
Swells in the agony of thy absence.

A latent lustre of the soul
Redefines Self.
The redeemer reverberates through
The golden grace of my guardian angel.

Server Down

Dementia of the developing-
Server down,
Slavery sucks.

Genuinity written off,
Bullied brains buried beneath
Sub-standard shades of sovereignty.

Insecurity

Shades of shame
Smell incessant insomnia,
Instigated by-
The reign of terror
        Or
The regression of refusal
        Or
A delusive demeanour;

That deconstructs the diaphragm
        Of
The golden globe
The oldest oncologist
The contented couple, or a singing soul.

On Misunderstanding

I climbed a cliff
      Stiff and steep-
To wake you up from slumber;

You woke and found
      No food around-
And thought I'm done with hunger.

Bankrupt

Bewildered, a bankrupt
Seeks shelter, shy.

Runs and runs-
With relentless pursuit of perfection.
Rewarded. Relaxed.

Borrowing burden
Breaks the broken.

The Beaten bankrupt
Bears the brunt
Of helpless hunger.

Lost and Found

Keys to happiness
Guilt stolen
By neurotic nepotism.

Niggling nightingale
Nips in the bud-
Nascent narrative numbers.

Sudden tsunami
Sang serene songs of success.
With Keys, submerged in the sea-bed!

Where are you?

Melancholy often moves
Thinking you are here,
          . . . but you are not.

Senses seldom sigh
Thinking you are here,
          . . . but you are not.

Slumber on the sly
Thinking you are here,
          . . . but you are not.

Dreams dearly dance
Thinking you are here,
          . . . but you are not.

Piercing pains falter
Thinking you are here,
          . . . but you are not.

Now what to do and where to go,
Psychic spells follow slow.
My pensive mind,
Tell where to find
The sunshine of my love . . .
O nights! No more,
The moon can score
Over a glimpse of: my Better-half.

We Don't Know Why

We don't know why
The sky's so high;
The then caterpillar
Is now a butterfly.

We don't know why
All hue-n-cry
For LGBT rights.
Sexual orientation- wherefore deny?

We don't know why
While one heart dries,
We pine for love.
But again the rights, the fights n bites,
Yelling alienation
And back to cries.

We don't know why
All people die.
Still we quarrel
And then sigh.

We don't know why
It's the Pain- that keeps us sane.
So more we try-
Not to cry-
While from the skies
The Omniscient smiless.

Raison d'etre

Aesthetic articulation
Befitting benevolence
Compassionate cohesion
Diligent diction
Earnest effervescence
Flowering feminism
God-fearing gratitude
Harmless hedonism
Insatiable insanity
Juvenile jealousy
Kind kisses
Lionhearted love
Mind-blowing mysticism
Noteworthy narrative
Octogenarian odyssey
Perennial potency
Quintessential quietude
Rejoicing resurrection
Soulful silence
Tender temperament
Unpretentious utterance
Virtuous visionary
Wondrous wisdom
XL Xmas
Yearning yin-yang
Zesty zephyr

Breathe In, Breathe Out

Breathe in
All that's fair;
Breathe out
Each nightmare.

Breathe in
All that's sane;
Breathe out
Pinching pain.

Breathe in
The fragrance of a flower;
Breathe out
The venom of power.

Breathe in
Every act kind;
Breathe out
Beasts of the mind.

Breathe in
The power of a prayer;
Breathe out
Those who don't care.

Breathe in
The Elysian nod;
Breathe out
All things odd.

Breathe in
The loyal promise of love;
Then rejoice with rewards-
And treasure thy Dove!

Breathe out
Temptations- They take your calm;
Now jump with joy-
For God is thy balm!

I fear Thee

I fancy facing you Nirbhaya *
Because I am a woman.
I am indebted to you
For your ailing eyes
That has sealed mine
Even before they coulde see
The death of yet another Nirbhaya
In the nearest mourning mirror.

I fancy facing you Nirbhaya
Because I am a man.
I pretend to have
Burried the beast
Between my balls
In the fear of being castrated amidst eunuchs.

But in the still of my solitude
Why can't I fake fearing you, O Nirbhaya?
Is that because
You have vowed vengeance
Through the octopus of
Hunger-free intestines, with none to lose?

My fear grows taller inch by inch
Of not having hung my head in shame
Since

The seed of blame
That bears no name
Bombards
With '*nir*' so lame, while '*bhaya*' the flame-
Of grotesque games
And cliché claims
Are crafted and cloned, time and again.

Nirbhaya in Hindi language means fearless [*bhaya*- fear, '*nir*'*bhaya*-
the fearless]

Here *Nirbhaya* is the name that was given by the city of New Delhi,
to the Paramedical student in India who died due to multi organ
failure after being brutally raped.

O Honey!

A little while ago,
I saw my Honey flow!

Let me tell you where,
In a teeming temple square!

The same icy eyes-
That goes beyond the skies;
The same lovely lips-
Where joyful jingle beeps;
The same hearty hair-
Clipped by mom with care;
The same hooray height-
She'd never let you fight;
The same sound of flute-
In all her scary shoot;
The same butter skin-
With *honey* flavored cream;
The same twitter talk-
While playing with the chalk;
The same naughty cry-
To snatch an apple-pie;
The same Hapi smile-
Sailing you to river Nile;
The same promise of *Jannat*-
Inside holy *Hindu* hummock!

Only one thing wasn't same,
This fairy had no fame-
Of '*W-o-w! Shukka-mam!*'

Come back once again,
To see me safe and sane,
My amber Honey, here's thy ardent fan!

Nothing Means More

There would never be another,
That could ever mean more,
Than-

Your graceful glance,
Your kind call,
Your genuine gestures,
Your love for all!

Your hearty health,
Your thankful thought,
Your honest order,
My gift that you bought!

Your concern and care,
In-depth and rare.
You aren't around-
 That's just not fair!

No money or fame,
Nor power game,
I pray to God,
While chant your name-
To give me *You*
Time 'n' again.

For-

There would never be another,

That could ever mean more,

Like the one who touched my soul,

And brought me Smiles- as none before.

Utopia

My joys knew no bound,
When my sweetheart I found!
After moving the world around,
After earning euro pound!

My sweetheart is a jolly man,
And joy for him is Peter Pan!
PG Wodehouse 'n' Jonathan Swift,
At the very first sight-
To him he'd gift!

My sweetheart is compassionate,
The reason why, he is my mate!
While other women die for a date,
My sweetheart says-
He loves his fate!

My sweetheart for sure,
Is my only cure!
When I say '*You are mine*',
Looks like he is- On cloud nine!

My heart and soul,
Seeks just no more,
He's my Utopia-
He's the Open door!

Comforting Combiflam

An anesthetic affection
Anchoring all angst and agony
Soothes to Sublime- the soul of sores.

A sound sleep spoils the sport.
Senses sulk,
Suppressed, silenced, censored.

Compassion, Compensatory

A vexed video of vice
Vested in the vicious circle
Of vengeance,
Mirrored the mood of
Vulgarism-
Vanquishing vanity;

Breathless breakdown
Virgin violated
Postmortem pulled:
Compassion compensatory.

Jeopardized Jealousy

The cheering chants of a champion
Channelized his chosen chums-
Cheated, Cheap.

Chirpy chats
Choked and chained a child-like.
Champion: clump-chucked.

Of False Accusations

Ruthless reasoning
Figures out furious flames
In the finest fiber of flowers...

Wild words
Wound the worldwide willingness
To weave a wishful welcome.

Cognizance confounds and consoles
The crooked curriculum:
Of ignorance and impotence, intertwined.

Keep in Touch

Rock-solid sounds of silence
Sheltered by
Shocking shells of pseudo-chauvinism
Seemingly sealed the sultry sea of senses.

Salt water seeped through
Surrounding sand speck,
Segmenting the soaring sea …

Intensified trauma
Testifies
The tormenting tide of truth.

Uncertified by Reason

My mind is inclined to believe
I'd see you again.
As a little child
Or just as now, once again
As my only little brother
Singing …………..
While my endless search for you would
Reverberate through your
Unbeatable rhythm.
You said you've searched everywhere
No city left undone.

My mind is inclined to believe
Our Bhagat carried similar message
Who knows where the search begins- and how futile the search.
Who knows he wasn't *Dadu*,
Pleading Sorry to my father through his flute?

My mind is inclined to believe
I'd see you again.
And this time my dearie
Extract painfully the 'you' from me;
Cause you'll be the elder sister and I the little brother,
The world will dance to reciprocate
To our current order …
Futility Dismissed- Search Sovereign!

Masquerade

Incorporeal incubation
Incorporated incredible incubus
Into indecisive yet indefatigable individualism.

Inchoate chaos culminated in
A curiously cultured curfew
Of kind kindred.

Creeping concussion breaks off with
Goofy gospels of grace.
Demarcated delusion. Masks misplaced.

The miasma of Inconsistency

Amidst the hurly burly in
A parrot fashioned paroxysm of hate
Jekyll and Hyde hyperactive.

Idiosyncratic ideologies ignite icebreakers
Hypnotherapy hush hush!
Implacable impact implanted.

Strangulated

The pinnacle of near perfection
Amongst the finest of the finite;
Playfully permeated the sense of sound
Like a veteran in the mode.

Increasingly, a sixth sense
Internalized the surrealistic sound system
Of nullifying numbskulls.

The current catatonic cataclysm inculcates
A claustrophobic Classical
That strangulates the cry of the catastrophe.

Diabolic Dad versus Father figure

The disdainful dance
Of disembodied devils
Devoured with deplorable depravity:
A divine decorum.
Daughter deconstructed.

The Fulcrum of Faith fulminates.
Fuming fear fosters
A fatalistic fortification of
The unfathomably fatigued father.

Fear not! Faded not!
Thy unfaltering, emphatic favor
O fastidious father figure!
Father's Day forthcoming.

Indispensible

That day at

Dawn
Shatter brained-
To part with
Your wisdom laden labour for me;
Your ever thriving thoughts for me;
Your blood turned water for me …

Dusk
Suicidal.
Parted with
Manifestations of your sacrosanct soul.

Darkness
Stoic.
Night-foss'icking, I grabbed
Your golden grace of Undeserved Mercy;
Selfishly for me, Mom.

Nuptials

When a child I dreamt of you
As a glossy red attire for my Barbie;
At teens I dreamt of you
As the blushing red of my 'red red rose',
As the recourse to my un-united soul.
And for now …
I dream no more
I stand with poise, firm;
With the glowing red soaring sun;
As a Dis-united whole.

Roars of Redemption

Deep down the dauntless daub
Of depression-
Crept a cruel cry
-Roaring for redemption.
Patient punctilious.

Post pacification,
The puritan
Perennially punishes pyromaniacs
-Roaring for redemption.

Proximity

Polluted proximity in portraits
Proclaim pangs of pain
Permeating pinching peace.

Pigeons prick the plight.
Purged Proximity- peels off pride!

Birth of a Storm

They parted with
Magnanimous warmth.
Conquered grief with grace,
Chaos with calm.
Two decades later,
One stormy night
She heard his drunken scream.
His sky scratching call
Did spark through her
Now contented soul.
Here began her haste
Of grabbing down
Thunder and Rains
From the salt soaking
Scratched Sky.
For she had seen
Labor pains promising-
The Birth of a Storm.

The Pervert

Obscene gesticulations made by
A hitherto respected octogenarian
Had Shaken the entire corridor of the
Fifty year old sacred shrine.
Perversion- they said.

While in sleep, the sicko shrieked,
Hungry- Hungry! Give me grains!
Hurry- Hurry! Bathe me in the rains!
Empty- Empty! They stole my brains!
Perversion- they said.

His boys and girls
Were busy at work
He waited for them
From dawn to dark.
While To and fro
He limped and lurched-
His thirsty gaze
For something searched.

Those dry eyes
Were blinded now,
They blocked his heart
And made a vow …

With stammering lips
Held fast to grief
Before he bid
His end goodbye,
He shrieked again
While fully awake
Then breathed his last
In the blink of an eye.

"To you old folks 'n' gentlemen,
To all my beloved brethren,
By the time you're seventy-nine
And you still feel all is fine,
To God Submit- Throw out thy hurt-
Else you senile, Die a pervert."